Stephen Lightbown is a Blac
disability rights champion.
1996 when he was sixteen,
voice to his disability. He 1
and at festivals such as {
Festival and Lyra Bristol Poetry ıᴄᴏᴜ.ᴀ.. _
has read internationally in San Antonio, Texas. His poems have
been widely anthologised, and *The Last Custodian* is his second
poetry collection.

'A compelling and formally inventive collection of poems that is also a sweeping story. Stephen Lightbown's *The Last Custodian* chronicles crisis, and questions our ideas of memory, survival. When towns become 'laden crematoriums', when tragedy takes everything, at that last moment, last stand: there is still a music. 'I have to hear a sound,' writes the poet, 'even if it's played / to photographs'. Coming, as it does, in this moment of global pandemic, The Last Custodian will touch many a reader with its unrelenting, questioning, echoing voice. A moving, inimitable book.'

Ilya Kaminsky,
author of Deaf Republic *and* Dancing in Odessa

'Stephen Lightbown's *The Last Custodian* complicates dystopian narrative by giving us a protagonist with a disability who explores an apocalyptic landscape in search of other survivors. Unspooling the narrative in searching, poignant poems and fragments that lovingly caress the details associated with the 'before times', Lightbown's work is reminiscent of 'The Comet', W.E.B. Du Bois's work of speculative fiction, where a black man and white woman find themselves, temporarily, the sole survivors of a catastrophe. As in Du Bois's work, Lightbown's dystopian landscape shines a light on how – in so-called 'normal' times – it's the marginalisation of people based on race and disability that is the real catastrophe.'

Ellen McGrath Smith, author of Nobody's Jackknife

'Stephen Lightbown's second collection *The Last Custodian* explodes with the force of myth. What would it be to be abruptly severed from the world as we know it? What would we learn, what would we discover? A compulsively readable narrative of survival, this book is also a revolutionary meditation on the construction of meaning and identity. Lightbown tells us, 'I've stopped straining my ears / to make out the words. The noise / is company enough.' These poems make you reconsider the axis of ability and disability and vision with wondrous urgency what it might take to move toward a wider vision of inclusion and connection. 'I know nothing of the road ahead,' Lightbown tells us. 'No helmet. No call from inside.' In joining him on this open road, we, too, are changed.'

Sheila Black,
co-editor of Beauty Is a Verb: The New Poetry of Disability

'Stephen Lightbown's post-apocalyptic poetic sequence takes us on a journey through a ravaged southern England, pointedly asking us: is that what it would take to make life as a wheelchair user better – the absence of others? An inverted quest full of bite and wisdom, *The Last Custodian* features ductile writing, with an enviable ability to quicken the blood.'

Rishi Dastidar

'Stephen Lightbown's The Last Custodian takes its reader on a journey through a strange but recognisable landscape, almost empty in the wake of catastrophe. En route we encounter airports, shops and pubs, decimated by a mysterious thickening dust. Through Luke, the custodian of the title, this collection shows us the real weight of loneliness and the vital hope that might keep us going. Travelling by wheelchair and motorway, he maps out a journey of survival that explores both the best and worst of humanity.

These poems are incredibly cinematic in their imagery, reminiscent at times of apocalyptic films such as 28 Days Later and The Road. This book is both bravely vulnerable and hearteningly playful. The Last Custodian quietly holds the everyday up to the light and makes us long for it; it asks what we could survive if we had to, and how that might change us.'

Suzannah Evans

The Last Custodian

Stephen Lightbown

Burning Eye

Also available by Stephen Lightbown
from Burning Eye Books:

Only Air

BurningEyeBooks
Never Knowingly
Mainstream

Copyright © 2021 Stephen Lightbown

The author asserts the moral right under the Copyright,
Designs and Patents Act 1988 to be identified as the author of
this work.

This edition published by Burning Eye Books 2021

www.burningeye.co.uk

@burningeyebooks

Burning Eye Books
15 West Hill, Portishead, BS20 6LG

ISBN 978-1-913958-07-7

The Last Custodian

Talking to a collection of stones,
I've already forgotten their faces.

how did I outlive you all?

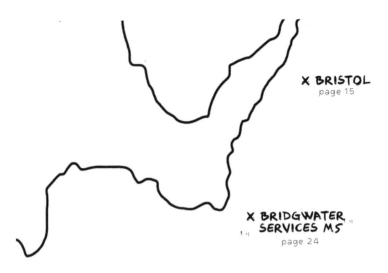

RAINHAM page 59
X

LONDON X
page 63

X
SWANLEY
page 58

CLACKET LANE
SERVICES M5 X
page 56

CANTERBURY
page 80
X

X GATWICK AIRPORT
page 54

SANDWICH
page 82
X

PEASE POTTAGE X
SERVICES M23
page 53

DOVER X
page 84

FOLKESTONE X
page 86

X PORTSMOUTH
page 44

X BRIGHTON
page 49

I

Day 1: Bristol

I drink the juice from the tinned peaches.
Gulp down survivor syndrome, ignore
the urge to add cream and lady fingers.
Thinking of dessert doesn't seem right
when I can't smile at you across our table
raised on four yoga blocks. A small ooze
of sugar water escapes from the tin
and settles in my beard. I leave it, fantasise
about an exhausted bee replenishing
itself on my chin. I wipe the sticky residue
away with a grubby hand. I'm so bereft
of contact that the thought of a bee
coming for pleasure, then leaving
to return to the hive, revitalised,
is simply too much.

Day 2: Bristol

Dear █████,
Your breath used to hibernate in my ear,
then crawl out of the woods to stretch.
I've waited for it to break through
the tree line…

Dear █████,
You used to sleep so beautifully,
a five-pointed star to curl around…

Dear █████,
From the window it looks like the world
has ended. I haven't seen anyone in weeks…

Dear █████,
You gave up work to bring me home,
nurturing this vegetable patch in a bucket
of sludge, chose to remain married.
Why won't you tell me: should I stay
here, with you, or leave?

Dear █████,
I have the attention span of your favourite mug.
I'll leave it outside the door. There's no
more medical supplies, the plants have died,
I've started drinking shampoo.
Somehow, I need to survive…

Dear █████,
This is goodbye. Today, I leave.
I will not take your name
out there with me.

Luke x

Day 4: Bristol

Freedom One: I was Danny Torrance
with his famous bowl cut, a back garden
in '84 and plastic slide. A seat scuttled
through the grass. Green trainers
a whir, riding with no helmet. Pedal
faster to become a better lap, Mum
calling from a window, *Time to come
in now.*

Freedom Two: Before dawn
and school registers I grafted for
escape on two wheels, a Diamondback
mountain bike. It gave me helter-skelter
hills, gravel grazes, Mars Bar lunches,
still no helmet. I had calves
carved like Michelangelo's David,
never braked for fear.

Freedom Three: Wheels
without pedals, constant
movement. The tarmac is mine.
I'm flirting. There is no one to respond.
Now I've got calves like David's
diminutive dick, but with woodcutter
forearms. I know nothing of the road
ahead. No helmet. No call from inside.

Day 8: Bristol

Take

only what you can carry
and drag.

Leave

everything else. Egg cups,
fridge magnets, the sofa
cushion mould of your
arse.

Leave

room for a hot water
bottle, tin opener, two pairs
of gloves, your inner
lava.

Leave

time to look around.
The smell of decay
won't obediently heel
when you close the door.

Leave

your fear of being alone.
There will be plenty
of new phobias to collect
along the way.

I've left

the way ███,
used to run her finger
along my surgery scar.

Take

care. I'm all that remains,
the claggy bottom of a
peanut butter jar.

Day 12: Bristol

Before, I never questioned
how a rocket went into space,
or how you made a pavlova.
That wasn't me.

I consider asking the bench
if it knows what happened.

On the seat
is engraved a name, Eric.
Why did the dust come?

He's silent,
like a four-year-old
would be if you challenged
her to split an atom.

Eric knows
as much as I do.

We are the world's
most eminent scientists.
I take the knife out of my bag,
scratch Dr before his name.

Happy graduation day, I say.

Day 14: Bristol

I'm sorry you're all dead.

At last I can leave
the house without
being spiked by jealousy.

I would see you

jog to work,
walk barefoot along
a beach collecting girlfriends,
fuck in a disabled toilet,
ride two horses bareback
through Wilko, chase
a lion scrapping with another
lion, use a clutch in a 1984
Mercedes convertible,
save a kite from a rainbow.

It's scary how free I feel
to not look at your
potential, wish
I could be the life
you took for granted

like breathing.

I would see you walk
from an argument
into an embrace.

Where's your air
now?

I want to say
I miss you –
all the things
we could have shared.

I would pick
our scab and
you'd feel it bleed.

Day 19: Bristol Airport

I think back to the first person I met in a chair who wasn't newly injured like me. He sat outside an artisan coffee shop with a metal cup and a hopeful smile. He wanted change. The sticker on his wheelchair said *DESERT STORM*. My new chair didn't have one, but if it did it would say *MOUNTAIN BIKE PUNCTURE*. I told him back in the UK people would assume car crash. I took the offered fist bump anyway. I felt like an imposter. That the respect wasn't deserved. We were comrades, though.

He told me in the States they respect their veterans.

I noticed his cup was empty.

Day 25: Bridgwater Services, M5

CLEAR UP BEGINS AFTER DUST STORM

The last headline.

It came. We didn't know
why Robert from Durham
spoke of Martian dust
hiding in the creases
of his washing. Farmer
Francesca complained
of shearing sheep dyed
candyfloss orange.

I grab a red top,
a Chomp, Peperami
and biro. Leave three
pebbles and a dandelion
leaf on the counter
because what's currency
now?

I look at the paper.
This historical document,
vacuum of pointlessness,
it told us nothing about
the poison to come.

Still, the crossword
will give me something
to do.

Day 30: Taunton Deane Services, M5

The driver's licence said her name was Eva.
The van she was driving said she delivered
for a meat wholesaler. The location said
this was where she would be laid to rest.

KeepCup on the dashboard, noise-
cancelling headphones on her head,
empty Tupperware box, bamboo spoon
on the passenger seat. Her own teeth
and nails collected in her lap.

Her last memory had been here
at a service station. I hoped
it had been a good one.
Perhaps flecks of paint
in the sky through a cheap
plastic telescope, not the
Eddie Stobart lorry
she had parked behind.

The car park was full of drivers
who had pulled over to digest
themselves, pool into their
footwells like a footbath
of their own liquifying
organs.

I took a scrap of paper and a pen
from the glove box. Placed
a eulogy under the windscreen
wiper. Turned the van
into a grave. The corpse
into a person.

HERE LIES EVA

Day 33: Clyst Honiton

I had come to find a toilet. Some cover, hopefully food,
a pint and a game of pool. I got four out of four. Swordfish
on tap, bag of Burts, polished cue ball, bathroom with running
Molton Brown. And a mystery. On the bar, a book. *Lone Wolf*,
by Jodi Picoult. Interest piñataed. A character called Luke, alone,
comatose. Left foot, right foot, header. A perfect hat-trick
of coincidences. The tagline: A life hanging in the balance.
I thumbed the pages like a Rolodex for more clues. A photo fell
from the last chapter. A woman. On the back a message.
There are more books like this. Titles with meaning. Keep moving.
It was signed, *The Librarian.*

Day 37: Torbay

Hospital inspectors would have walked the path I do.
The main entrance, first observations: the floor

stained with prayers, could do with a clean, pile of corpses.
Bayview Coffee Bar shuttered in a Styrofoam of death.

Everyone will need to take their final breath,
safe care provided, pillows, a last rite handed out.

Did it feel like wandering the trenches with a lantern,
applying gauze and a prayer to amputated limbs?

They would have done it though, carried on, call bells,
exploding like missiles; nurses would not have known

what they were running towards, their own fate,
clear as flashing orange warheads in ceiling tiles.

Bed after bed without answers until they stopped,
fell still, with the pulse of their small watches.

Outpatients, pharmacy, A&E, I find what I need
from the pockets of the new earth.

Cause of death,
the same.

Day 40: Plymouth

The sky is peeling.

Visibility measured
by abandoned cars.
This day is three
Golf Estates thick.

There is a strange beauty
in the red that stains
the sky. Cinematic,

almost; yesterday's tarmac
is still in the palm of my hands.
Dust rents my lungs.

My static day marked
by disappearing tyre tracks.
Every wasted breath

trashes my chances
of meeting the Librarian.
I need some sort of purpose.

Hope scratched
by the grit from
the constant cloud.

No choice but to wait,
reeking of cherry juice
and paranoia.

Movement is futile. A sign
in an abandoned Subway:
More freshly made tomorrow.

Day 41: Plymouth

I turn into the street. The familiarity of potholes under wheels gives me hope that this one may have been exempt. I see the postbox where Mum would post my birthday and Christmas cards. I push to it, put my hand in its mouth, place a palm where she would have placed hers, to hold her hand before…

I ask the postbox, *Has she been here, has she tried to write?*

The postbox doesn't reply. I look down at the dust and see only my tyre tracks, no footprints. I could post my faith somewhere else.

I decide to hold on to it.

Day 42: Plymouth

I find them in their double bed, insides by insides. Dad loved the way you could lift up the mattress and reveal a huge storage space underneath. I want to hold them, but I can't bear to touch, see, smell. Eventually the bed will take them.

When people die they look like they're sleeping. That's a lie. They don't look peaceful at all; they look dead, not like my parents.

I'm glad you were together, I whisper at the husks I can't recognise.

Before I leave, I wonder if they ever felt this helpless when they watched me in a hospital bed. Altered from the son they raised, but still their son – a seed into a tree, into a table, then a bonfire.

I place a framed picture of them on the side of the bed, their faces held together by the light.

Day 45: Kingsbridge

Talking to a collection of stones,
I've already forgotten their faces.

Grandad is late out of my
North Face rucksack.
A large *G*, now tattooed
in Sharpie on his cliff face.

U and I never got time to talk
about having a child. One of those
conversations that gets ignored,
a cobweb in a lampshade.

The rest of my family:
*M*um, *D*ad, *N*an.
Their own letters weigh heavy;
how did I outlive you all?

Removing the remainder
of the contents – flask,
goggles, cable ties –
placing them all in the cart,
dragging this caravan of life.
It carries medication, a way
only into tomorrow.

I'm low on catheters, laxatives,
a day or so as dust falls
from the next hospital.

Addressing the family: *I can't
push Chair through a silence.*

Day 46: Start Point Lighthouse

When I was newly injured *M* would bring me to this mile of jutting headland punctuated with a lighthouse. We would come early; I didn't want the pity of ramblers, offers of help, witticisms or indifference. In truth, it was my own expectations I wanted to avoid; I'd compare myself to them. I wanted strangled ankles from tightly wound walking boots, the jolt of cliff stones under foot. Even the hill sheep with their freedom and parkour couldn't escape my judgement. *M* would hold the rucksack that would become her home as I zigzagged my way up the mile of self-esteem. Narrow the angles but increase the distance; this path was about learning trade-offs. Back here, with *M*. I sense her silently nurturing once more. I never questioned the encouragement, just went forwards. Maybe I needed to find my balance in the void. Halfway up the hill. Framed by a field of ferns, I'm OK with stopping. I follow the gaze of the lighthouse.

Moving with purpose
Towards the shore that hits back
I see a future

Day 52: Torquay

That's all we are:
hunted, prey.
Hands around my mouth,
pulled to the ground.
I am no threat.
Cheek to gravel.
I see my wheels disappear.
Instinct takes over.
Find *G*, the slingshot.
See the impact. Temple implodes.
Am I prey or hunter now?

We are both on the floor,
unable to move.

Unable to move,
we were both on the floor.

Am I prey or hunter now?
Saw the impact. Temple implodes.
Found *G*, the slingshot.
Instinct took over.
I saw my wheels disappear.
Cheek to gravel.
I was no threat.
Pulled to the ground.
Hands around my mouth.
Hunted,

                  prey.

Day 54: Torquay

I want to lie under the rubble
of a fallen wall, to understand
the weight of unknown faces.

I hold *G* in my hand.
Remember watching him
clean blood from gutted fish
in his garage.

What I have done still smeared
across his surface.

Is this how it is now? I ask.
One against one. Can I do that?

Day 55: Torquay

The first thing I notice is the smell –
rancid horses' stable.

It lingers like the 3am guest at an old party.
I find her in the front room with the armchairs.

She could have been forty. Her perfume
despair. I guess a week, if not longer.

Is that you, John? Her words catch
in a riptide looking for the shore.

I keep my eyes open for signs. Two rucksacks,
one rolled-out mattress, a book, *Don Quixote*.

Her voice in the cushions, swollen,
bandaged, clearly a ruin.

Did you find him, that man in the wheelchair?

John. The man I killed.

I hold back the urge to gag. To cry. To leave.
I move towards her, place my hands on
something I'm still trying to understand.

II

Day 71: Honiton '

i could call a cat a meowopotamus,
who would care?

and yet, as the sun clambers,
i've stayed as Luke.

i took the life of another,

Luke.

when i was four days old,
when i was three eye blinks
post-surgery.

when he asked me my name
                Luke.

he drawled each letter
L   u   k   e

it felt euphoric, maybe erotic,
to hear someone say my name,

to know who i was, to stay who i was.

i'd always quite liked the name Tyler,
        i met one once in California,

he ate white rice
        with raw eggs and walnuts for breakfast.

        i could never have been that guy.

when i was given a wheelchair,
        still Luke

when i met, then lost *u*,
        still Luke

today,

        despite every wretched contortion,

        still   Luke.

Day 75: Chickerell

My dead skin mixes with their
dead skin. I transfer onto the sofa,
an exchange of unpleasantries,
asleep in less time than it takes
to say *viva las Chickerell*, awake
not long after. The sound of
the fridge opening, I'm here
alone with a single jar of
mayonnaise floating into
the room that died three
months ago, a box of *Happy
Families* lunges at me, a pair
of Crocs cartwheel in my
direction. Something prods
me from behind. The ghosts
of this bungalow want
my attention. I've stopped
knocking before I enter
houses; maybe that was
the wrong thing to do.

What's the matter, lad?
You afraid of the dodgems?
You too small for this?
he says through a fag.

I want to get off.

Day 80: Dorchester

I cross Grey's Bridge near the teddy bear museum,
arrive into a Rothko exploration on canvas.

The countryside behind me, this is nature unsettling.

The sky is thriving. The dust, orange in midday sun;
where it lingers in shadows, a darker red.

The lines have been erased; buildings are a blur.
Consumed by technicolour.

The depth of the street only revealed with every
roll I make further into the painting.

After the bridge, I fall into a palette of emotions.

The dust paints the hairs on my arms orange.
My trainers turn red. Trousers. Wheels. Red.

The orange of my T-shirt meets the red
of my wasteland.

I have been painted into today.
I close my eyes. For once it isn't black.

Day 82: Bournemouth

New York, June 2014. On the High Line we sat and watched the yellow procession on Tenth Avenue make its way to Kong's last stand. *U* held a painting of a wiener dog we'd just bought from a street vendor. He asked where we were from. When we said London, he replied, *Man, that place, I freaking love a Nando's.* I held a cinnamon bun in one hand and paid with the other. I asked *U* if the fact grilled chicken was a reason someone came to our capital city was something we should be proud of. I'd wanted to tell him all the other reasons why he should visit, but nothing came to mind. *Why protect a place you've spent this trip running away from? U* had a point. A man wearing a Yankees cap spoke in German as he herded his family into position for a portrait. Click. Beep. Click. Beep. Click. Beep. Click. Beep. Click. The fake shutter noise wrestled for attention with the car horns. We didn't need a camera to capture any of this. (Can *U* still remember? Wherever *U* are. All these details are so vivid, yet I can barely recall *Ur* face.) Below we were drawn towards a man in a blue hard hat and high-vis vest. We watched him stand in the middle of the road and wave passengers from sidewalk to sidewalk. Functioning with deactivated nuclear energy. I tried to see from the way he waved his flag whether he was bored or fulfilled. I told *U* I'd take any job just to live here. Not one pedestrian acknowledged the man or the flag. I wanted to shout down, say anything. There was attitude on every corner, but I had never seen *U* so serene. I had a taste for *Ur* maxi dress, a dizzying devotion. It was the colour of absinthe and somehow was calm in the breeze coming off the Hudson. Old Blue Eyes was right; I did want to be a part of it. I looked for more dollars. The feeling was ferocious. I went back to see if I could buy more hours in that day.

I need to find a breath to go again.

Day 97: Portsmouth

I smoothed the tablecloth,
grateful this wouldn't be a dinner
for one. It was an act. I'd been
minutes from pulping the napkin
with my hands. I wasn't brave
enough to look up; not yet,
at least.

I kept focussed on the descent.
U could have been a stray
boulder, the kind that would
eat me from the saddle, graze
every part I'd exposed.

Luke? It's me, ██████*, are you going
to say hello?* I blanked the face
I didn't yet know. *Hello,* I replied,
eyes still down, waited

for a conversation to become
lost in the dark.

Day 100: Portsmouth

There are things I thought I would miss
but don't. Like the way I thought I'd be
desperate to fuck when I lost my legs,

but all I wanted was to hold my wife
and run my fingers over her like she was
a blade of grass I didn't want to bend.

The only difference between a
creeping speedwell defiantly in a lawn
and a hyacinth in a hand-painted vase
is the care it was placed with.

My urge to tend the weeds is strong.
I want to tell them, wherever *U* are,
U grow in all the right places.

Day 102: Portsmouth

I was eight when I saw my first dead body. Our neighbour in Plymouth. Heroin. Surrounded by the dead all I'm thinking about is corpses I've seen before. We lived in a big townhouse down near the marina. The super yachts looked like model boats from my bedroom. Next door had been converted into flats. This guy lived on the top floor. Nice bloke. Always in a pair of cycling shorts. I used to help him clean his mountain bike. He'd tip it upside down. I'd furiously spin the pedals whilst he dripped oil on to the chain. I went at those pedals like I was hand cranking a Model T Ford. I got into biking because of him. It was guilt. I wanted to keep his bike on the road. People asked us how we didn't notice he was missing. New tenants kept arriving. For a week or so I remember a smell moving into our house. The way **N** did when **G** was in hospital with a disease I couldn't pronounce. The memory of it made me sad. We couldn't place it. Out of the window I remember seeing a shadow of white boiler suits walking up and down the stairs on the outside of the building. Next thing the boiler suits are carrying a stretcher with a body bag. The smell went with him.

Day 112: Chichester

A bird arrives, nonplussed.

The sky has been silent for weeks.

I am hungry for this bird,
a collared dove,

not for the meat under its wings,
but the company.

Does this bird know the end
of the world is here?

I do not speak, remain plastic
café table still.

Time is too precious
to waste on sudden movements.

Its only interest in me is the food
I cannot offer. Its funeral eyes

mirror my own.

I wonder if those eyes watched
as its mother spoke,

You can be an eagle.

Its head bobs like it's listening
to dirty beats, wing propped on a bar.

I offer my filthy hand,

crave the dance contact brings.

Let me stroke this bird,
each feather a friend lost.

I'm here, I'll barter Carnation milk
for conversation.

I watch it fly; my red circles
chase it through the dust.

Day 120: Brighton

Following the trail is like driving a Grand Prix track in a cardboard box, address written on the top. Delivery drivers on their tea break, but the kettle has been stolen, so they go to the café next door, which is shut, then out comes the whisky; no driving today. And I'm sat in the box waiting for a delivery slot whilst the other cars hiss by. Lap after lap. I have been denied death. Again. Every once-able soul is somewhere else and I cannot get in. It would've been nice to have a free run at the aftermath, but for every door with level access there is a whole town of ring pull tuna up a flight of stairs. I'm no supercrip to be wanked over. I'm just trying to break the tape.

Day 122: Brighton

Remember when I was chair
height and would bring
home a feather if I saw one
on the street?

Tape it to a teddy
until I had a bird bear.
Give it wings, watch
it fly away from my
hugs.

As an adult I'd watch a seagull
strut. I'd look at its plumage,
think, that bird

has dined on a drain-drunk rat,
then rummaged landfill
for a dessert of thrown-out
Micro Chips and used
nappies.

***M**, why didn't you say anything?*
Why did you let me pick up
those feathers?

Am I making sense?

I've started
collecting feathers
again. I need help
finding a bear.

Day 123: Brighton

I killed another man today.
Over a book. *The Da Vinci Code.*
Go figure. The Lanes are stained
with his blood. I take him
on my tyres.

Day 129: Brighton

It has all gone to shit.
I don't know which way is home.
I'm using an empty packet
of Quavers as a compass.

If ██████ were here I would let
her eat the needle.

I'd fill the empty bag
with gravel if it meant I could
share something with her again.

I look at the packet. Beg it
to direct me back to the sofa
with her, season three of Ozark
and cheese dust.

Day 138: Pease Pottage Services, M23

Everybody is busy being dead. But I see you, carrier bag caught in the branches of a tree grown with sorrow at these last-piss services.

Small twig fingers grasp your handles. Even you just want to be held. To feel the weight of being useful. You made it past the dead. Just like we were warned. A breeze catches, your plastic flutters like a sob.

I too take in air, behind me, for once too much to bear. Frozen as though a lost internet connection and I'm a glitch. I should have been a kite, you would say as you climbed free on the wind, and then: trapped. Back to bag.

I anchor to those images, buoys in the ocean. There will be more bags, caught in the embrace of a tree. Will anybody listen?

I reach for the tree
Even here I cannot climb
I swim from the buoy

Day 140: Gatwick Airport

In lieu of a passport I wave a used plaster
at the check-in desk. *I'm off to Wroclaw,*
I shout at a recycling bin. I carry a suitcase
through security, hold my arms out for
a cold feet pat-down that never shows,
my kills paraded in a clear bag.
Breeze through duty-free, do not turn left.
Good day to you, impossibly smooth flooring.
I unhook the cart from the back of Chair.
And push. I glide like a curling stone, imagine
a pleasant chap in black pants sweeping
a path before me. The remains of weekend
revellers cheer, gate after gate. An empty
airport is a ridiculous place. As many toilets
as planes on a runway. I take a pilot cap off
a corpse. I'm a pilot now, almost useful.
Potentially respectable. *This is your captain
speaking; we are beginning our descent.*
I let that lie soar through Terminal 2.

Day 142: Somewhere on the M23

There is a callus for every landmark.
So many points of uninterest, rest
days become procrastination.
Stonehenge in a rucksack. I stop only
when my hand tells me to.

Mark my aching map with pins
and needles. I stay when tomorrow
looks pointless. Line of love, line of
head, line of life.
M3, M4, M5.

Tonight, I'll sleep in a layby on my palm,
by a burger van with forgotten beef.
Opening the pages of my hand,
remembering the emptiness
of fields.

My voice, unfamiliar as horses in
a cinema. Somewhere along my thumb
is an endpoint. I'll find it when the dust
clears.

My wedding ring taps like a metronome.

Day 146: Clacket Lane Services, M25

The frame of a wheelchair, if drawn in lines, looks
like a section of a flight of stairs. I notice this now
for the first time as I take the wheels off to clear
them of memories. When assembled, the frame
has two wheels at the back, the size of dustbin lids
(ones without wheels), and two wheels at the front,
the size of the palms of my hands. The frame itself
used to be a polished silver; now it's scratched,
dull, held together with gaffer tape and hair ties.
Chair has pushed past the remains of a country
that only a year ago would have stood on two feet
and thought I could not survive without help.
How far would I have made it without this frame,
these four wheels?

Day 148: Shoreham

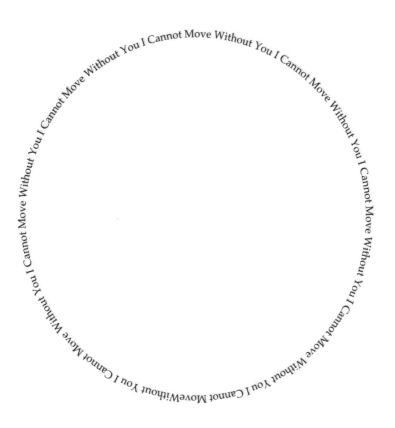

Without You I Cannot Move Without You I Cannot Move Without You I Cannot Move Without You I Cannot Move Without You I Cannot Move Without You I Cannot Move Without You I Cannot Move Without You I Cannot Move Without You I Cannot Move Without You I Cannot Move Without

Day 154: Swanley

Allen key. Tennis ball. Wrists, bent elbows. I wear pain.
Connected like asteroids in orbit. The impact is their pain;

they won't let go. Hold it like a child's hand on a
hard shoulder, *take two of these, it will help bear pain,*

and I want to sleep with the lamp on. It stays on the bedside
table, unquestionable; at least some parts still share pain.

I dial the number for agony. Engaged, I bruise lines
under jeans, left to right, back again, a secret, to repair pain

now out of reach, a dad in a wheelchair; beauty haunts
my landscape. Small faces. Tears. They scare pain

with a single letter written on a stone, *u*, not just a capital.
Become the past. A hill of scalpels to prepare pain.

Doorbell. Junk mail. Headstones. These towns are laden
crematoriums. Luke, it's yours, a gift. Everywhere, pain.

Day 181: Rainham

Voices at the bus stop, idly
chatting at an aloe vera baggage
carousel in the Good Housekeeping
waiting room, shouts of

well done, mate as I push up a hill,
comments, jokes, rejections, the same
can you do a wheelie? question
I've heard four hundred and twelve
times before.

And I hate
that I miss it all.

I'd trade my cracked
voice

talking with a family of stones
for one tinder strip comment
that would deliver rage.

Do you want a hand with your bag?

At least my breath would still
exist in their world.

I'd barter it all
for one last whisper, under
the weight of an Egyptian cotton
bedsheet from ▇▇▇

I see you.

I see you.

Day 194: Barking

We clinked IPAs
to better things.

I didn't believe in toasts.
U did. We took a bottle top each,
a memento of our pledge. Looked up;
I was always surrounded by giants.
Wrapped in blankets, wrapped in hope.
I carried the bottle top. Held it
against my ear. It spoke to me.

It said drink up the hope,
made with fresh hope, hope
on tap, you'll get addicted
to hope, real craft hope, two
hopes for the price of one,
award-winning hope.

U said it tasted like
clean clothes and optimism.
It tasted like overpriced
beer to me.

We had a drink to better things.

Why did the bottle top choose me?
It told me to push.
All those giants knew nothing.
Where's their hope now?

I carried that hope for seven years.
Buried it in the ground. Outlived it.
I carry a stick now. Trained it to beat
any remaining hope out of me.
I'm empty. Bigger than the giants.

III

Day 200: London

I understand.
Here, now, I can draw
a zip around it all, the sky
is canvas, this one-man tent
of a world. I am alone, with every
mistake I have ever made
and no one to own up to.

Day 207: London, The British Library

The ceiling rises upwards
as if the year escaped the first day.
I've traipsed my finger along a spine
from Bristol.

I don't know why I'm here.
She watches, her back to the
box office. She's assumed
control. I have to decide if I'm
returning or borrowing something.

It's a bit bigger than Waterstones.
That was the best I could do.
I'd wanted to see a face, her face,
the Librarian.

I'm trying to build the world
with books. And here you are,
you made it, you followed?
Now what do you do?

She had spoken through pages.
Brought me here to show
we would not start
from scratch.

High-rise stories
and no one
to listen.

I can't flick to the truth.

It's OK, she says. *In amongst*
everything we got wrong
are all the things we almost
got right. It won't be
easy; it never was.

Day 211: London

I've started writing assistance
on my shopping lists.
There are words without
lines through them. Cake,
gingham curtains, pity.

From before. When I wheeled
through a door I collected
disappointment. My differences
clearer than lifeboats
at a rodeo.

I recall their questions, not faces.
Do you need a hand with that?

I'll let you know.

Now. I see myself in the gradual
revolutions of fusilli pasta.
I clear shelves, my hands reach
to write messages in cards
no one will read.

In these bemused aisles,
can I be disabled if there's
no one to compare me to?

Day 216: London, Piccadilly

The Coca-Cola lights are forlorn.
Bereft of shoppers, bumping shoulders
in cashmere wishlists. Like dogs
that keep eating as long as there's food.

Fattening bags with empty gestures
that won't be acknowledged by
New Year's Eve. Every house I've been in
seems full of plastic declarations.

Christmas Eve, and I'm searching
for something that will make tomorrow
different. I throw a street cone through
the window of Fortnum & Mason,

take a basket. A cured glazed ham
covered in promise, honey-roasted cashews,
three bottles of solitude remover. Dinner.
I will light a Cohiba Talisman
for making it this far.

Day 220: London

That she's had a haircut is distressing.
There is a white band between hairline
and skin. It laughs at me like a crooked
smile along the south. When I woke this
morning I didn't think to make an effort.
Wasn't being *here* enough?

My matted hair of bungalows
feels like bramble to my fingers.
If you were to find cabbage, I'd bare
my neck to twelve nibbling hamsters
if it meant I could have a trim.

There's a hint of a fade, product,
sculpting, artistry. I want to hang
her head in the Tate. It still surprises
what can make me unsettled.
I point, my finger a divining rod,
her hair water on Mars. *Not now*,
she says. *Listen*.

Day 228: London

It is ten years since
we lived here.

1.
A spray-painted hedgehog
on a locksmith wall. A lane
of bricks takes us east. We walk
towards unpronounceable
cocktails in a repurposed
petrol station.

2.
U lean down to kiss me
at London Bridge. A tourist
ignores the skyline to
capture our embrace.

3.
Underneath a blanket,
on a sofa. A secret screen.
James Stewart told us
how wonderful it was.

4.
Kicked out for doing
backstroke. We were trying
to eat the rooftops in
London Fields like Pac-Man
chasing ghosts.

5.
We crashed a party
for those who passed the bar,
now asleep on the bar.
Waiters dressed as elves
served eggnog and wished
only us a Merry Christmas.

6.
Just off the Strand,
the *Lion King* poster looks
at me again. Watching
as I touch the exhibits.

Day 254: London, The British Library

I stroke the cover of every book she has given me. I'm tugged to the ones with the broken spines, wonder if they've spent their lives trying to prove they are still books.

She hands me a copy of *Madame Bovary*.
Give this to the Bibliothécaire.

She tells me I can come back, that, now I know there are others, I need to understand if this is it. Always expectations. I want to ask why this isn't enough. I want to thank her for guiding me. I want to hold her, feel the warmth of someone other than me, but don't.

I accept the book, draw an **L** on the gift with my Sharpie. She takes the pen from me. *You don't need this.*

She points at Chair. *Stop pushing from your reality.*

Day 255: London, Kings Cross

1. Gustave Flaubert.
Madame Bovary, 1856.
We screwed the earth, so it
bit back. We didn't understand
it was language that separated
us from nature. So it was taken.
I'm here because we still need
custodians. There is a debt
to pay. A single note: *Luke is not brave,*
or sent to inspire. He knows how.
The Librarian.

2. Andy Weir.
The Martian, 2011.
I am Watney, trowel
in hand, ready to grow potatoes
in my desperation. Perhaps
everyone left me behind.
Hello. A single note:
When you are ready,
come. Find the frequency;
I am listening. The Librarian.

3. Elmore Leonard.
Unknown Man No. 89, 1977.
Year I was born. On the counter
of WHSmith. Admirable man,
under stress, adrift, becomes whole.
Never get personally involved.
A single note: *Move on.*
The Librarian.

4. Edwidge Danticat.
Everything Inside, 2019.
I saw the beacon.
Approached, cautious; I only
creak. Laid out like kindling,

eight copies, eight stories,
coming to terms with
a dance between old, new.
A single note: *It seems*
so big, yet each journey is intimate.
The Librarian.

5. Regina Porter.
The Travelers, 2019.
Interconnected. Resetting.
Generations driven by memories.
Barriers, pain, love, family.
This is not one story.
A single note: *The pages will*
come together. The Librarian.

Day 267: London

Trouble in the
distance; it can wait
for now. Sea, take me
as I am. Erode the desire
from my bones. Let the
salt scrub me clean.

IV

Day 273: Somewhere on the M20

You stop to admire
the horses, beyond
the SOS phone.

You imagine
they are sleeping.

Some freedom,
ahead.

Day 276: Somewhere on the M20

Things I did not expect to see today.

1. A man.

To be precise, a naked man
running with a pair of sandals
threaded through a leather
belt round his waist.

He was on the other side
of the central reservation.
In the outside lane, a few
years short of seventy.

I twitch towards the knife
gaffer-taped to Chair.

He gets nearer, whistling
a tune I can't quite make out.

How are flashers still a thing?

He sees me.
Without missing a stride, he vaults
the barrier between us. I wince.

That tune. Louder. Clearer.
Aerosmith, 'I Don't Want to Miss a Thing'.

He comes to a standstill.
Everything static; well, almost.
He looks like a grandfather clock
with a pendulum cock.

Tattooless. Hairless (goatee aside).
Chatty. *Greetings to you.*

I mean you no harm,
just out for a run.

                                        Mate.
                            You don't know
                        the danger you are in.

What from, where to? I ask.

Nowhere, just a run.

I have to know.
Why no clothes?

The serrated edges of the knife
call to me. Only gaffer tape
is saving him.

Look around, my good friend.
I'm the least of your worries.

Day 280: Canterbury

I remember calm and I stop, roll *U* over the skin
on my left shoulder, and *U* are there kneeling
behind me on our bed, and I feel *U* push *Ur* fingers
into the places I don't want to go. And I remember
calm as the smell of cloves from cheap massage oil
dripping into the sheets. And I pilot *U* over tender
fingerprints left on me, desperate to smooth out
the octopus that has nestled on the seabed.
And *U* would whisper, I carry the distance in the spool
of my sockets and calm is somewhere in the reel
of tangled wire. I remember calm as *U* would say
if I find myself somewhere I can't push from
then I should hold *Ur* touch, massage *U* deeper
into the tissue, count off each mile to calm.

Day 315: Sturry

He used to call me King Luke.
The first time *D* hid his disappointment
I was fourteen, kicking a ball against a wall
when I should have been weighing cauliflower.
A petrol smoothie had more appeal. Occasionally
I would help out; I'd hear him whistling
Gilbert and Sullivan whilst arranging oranges.
It made me want to press thumbs into
my eyes, bruise them like an apple skin.
I wasn't made for heavy labour; I was barely
made to be an adequate son. At school
I'd imagine swapping places with friends;
any one of them would've been better
suited to eulogising yoghurt raisins.
I carried his sadness when it would have
been easier to ask about the perfect time
to sell a persimmon, but the question
never came naturally, like the trade
was meant to do, like being alone
has come to me.

Day 333: Sandwich

I spent the afternoon chatting
to *G* about his garage; it smelt of petrol,
solitude and graft. This one smells of potpourri;
it seems out of place. I consider the freezer
– large, silent, probably stuffed with
disappointment. I don't want to open it.
The tender imagination of potato waffles,
fish fingers, Viennetta is better than a starter
of power-downed mush.

I distract myself by interrogating the displaced
dining room chair familiarly covered in gaffer tape,
stroke the tape tacked against Chair.
I can't look any more without knowing
the meal I could have had. Between melted peas,
something not bought from Iceland nor any
shopping list I ever made. A severed head.
Eyes open, mouth closed. Male, over fifty.
Still wearing glasses. *We need to leave*, I say to *G*.
I'll get the others. I've become used to death.
This, though, is brutal. I close his eyes,
the freezer lid, thoughts of dinner.

Day 340: Finglesham

I talk to the wind,
always trying to make itself
heard through the trees.
Tongue of branches, voice
undecipherable, an instruction,
                a warning,
                      a paragraph of profanities.

I've stopped straining my ears
to make out the words. The noise
is company enough.

Day 356: Dover

I'd heard stories about these arms that follow
you home. Long since dismembered, hunting
in packs. The advice is clear. DON'T FEED THE ARMS.
Calloused digits that move slightly. Covered in tattoos
of ex-lovers' names. Gravel grazes, torn-off flesh
that swings like a fat cat's cat flap.

I saw one once. It was caught in the polluted
blackberries of the bramble. I made no attempt
to free it. Left my own arms by my side.
It was grey, still, like a ravaged rattlesnake.

Streaky bacon forearm. Elbow malevolent mauve.
Bluebottle knots where a shoulder should be.
On closer inspection, it was (perhaps) filthy.
A single arm can't wash itself. Can it?
Now I lie in bed with a death row conscience,
thinking I hear it tap Morse code at the window:
Let me in.

Whenever I leave the house, I worry it will be there.
Up on its hind knuckles. Thumb and forefinger
formed as a mouth. Panting through its blood
smear lips. A muscled index finger a mottled
wand of misadventure. No magic. Only fear

always shuffling behind me. Chuntering.
Words caught behind thick scabs and fury.
Desperately trying to make its point. Until
it lunges at my throat. Embalms my
nostrils. It has no eyes.

It will not see me smile.

Day 364: Folkestone

I think this is where we say goodbye, I say to ███ as I take her in my hand. I marvel at her in my past, notice that some of the Sharpie line has been smudged, most likely from tears and morning kisses. I wait for something in return. I smile. *It's OK, **U** don't have to say anything. Just being with me has been enough.*

I've already dug a hole. The others are in there. *M* rolls towards *D*; is it a sob or sigh? They all face up, take one last look at the orange sky. This time I want them to know what's coming, to come to terms with it before it happens.

I ask if she's ready, place my discreet whispers against her grey granite surface, then gently lower her. I sweep the earth over my family, let them disappear.

Day 365: The Channel Tunnel

The weight of the Channel takes its toll
on my shoulders. A body is not built to carry
the sea, even one that could be held
in a glass. The antiseptic cleanliness of
darkness conjures the idea that the year
of death is nothing more than sugar
dissolved in tea. There, but only if you think
about it. At Point Median, between Folkestone
and Coquelles, I focus on a memory.
Foreplay after cheesecake. Wonder
for a second if that memory could be
a premonition. I know now I am lost. A voice
can disappear without ears to receive
and it's tiring to realise this could be it.
The menace of the water above is heavier
than I expected. If this tunnel is the cheesecake,
I'm not sure I want the gentle stroking
at the other end. My eyes falter, as if
I had a choice. It starts to take me under.
Is this what free feels like? I call out,
Where are you?

Je suis là.

Acknowledgements and Thanks

Thanks to the editor of Dreich Magazine, where versions of some of these poems have appeared.

Thanks to Suzannah Evans, Anthony Anaxagorou and Ellen McGrath Smith for their support, cajoling, encouragement and wisdom as mentors through the writing of these poems; to the whole wonderful team at Burning Eye for continuing to let me share my poetry with the world; to Kate Hazell for the incredible artwork on the cover and within this collection; to the Hours group for your kind and always helpful critique; to every disabled poet whose words deserve to be read and shared, and to Carly for letting me sit at the desk to write hundreds of drafts of poems and then reminding me to close the laptop as it was my turn to make dinner.

9 781913 958077